Mediterranean Salads Cookbook

Fresh and Flavorful Recipes Inspired by the Mediterranean Diet

MEDITERRANEAN SALADS COOKBOOK

First edition. November 17, 2023.

ISBN: 979-8223306221

Written by Sammy Andrews.

Table of Contents

Sammy Andrews

Chapter Outline:

Introduction to Mediterranean Salads

- The Mediterranean Diet: A Healthy Way of Life
- The Beauty of Mediterranean Salads

Essential Ingredients

- Olive Oil: Liquid Gold of the Mediterranean
- Vinegars, Herbs, and Spices
- Fresh Produce: The Heart of Mediterranean Salads

Classic Greek Salads

- Traditional Greek Salad (Horiatiki)
- Greek Pasta Salad with Feta
- Greek Couscous Salad

Italian Delights

- Caprese Salad: Tomatoes and Mozzarella
- Panzanella: Tuscan Bread Salad
- Insalata di Riso: Italian Rice Salad

Spanish Sensations

- Gazpacho Salad
- Ensalada Mixta: Mixed Spanish Salad
- Salmorejo: Creamy Tomato and Bread Soup Salad

Middle Eastern Inspirations

- Tabouleh: Fresh Herb and Bulgur Salad
- Fattoush: Lebanese Bread Salad
- Moroccan Chickpea and Couscous Salad

Mediterranean Protein-Packed Salads

- Tuna Niçoise Salad
- Grilled Chicken and Quinoa Salad
- Lentil and Roasted Vegetable Salad

Refreshing Seafood Salads

- Shrimp and Orzo Salad
- Calamari Salad with Lemon and Herbs
- Mediterranean Octopus Salad

Vegan and Vegetarian Creations

- Mediterranean Chickpea Salad
- Roasted Eggplant and Red Pepper Salad
- Spinach and Walnut Salad

Inventive Salad Dressings

- Lemon-Tahini Dressing
- Pomegranate Vinaigrette
- Honey Mustard Yogurt Dressing

Salads for All Seasons

- Summer Watermelon and Feta Salad
- Autumn Harvest Salad
- Winter Citrus Salad

Sides and Complements

- Homemade Pita Bread
- Tzatziki and Hummus
- Stuffed Grape Leaves (Dolmas)

Salad Presentation and Garnishes

- Artful Plating
- Edible Flowers and Herbs
- Nut and Seed Crunch

Mediterranean Salad Bowls

- Building the Perfect Salad Bowl
- Breakfast Salad Bowl
- Buddha Bowl

Salads for Special Occasions

- Wedding and Celebration Salads
- Picnic and Potluck Favorites
- Date Night Dinner Salads

Mediterranean Salad Etiquette

- Cultural Considerations
- Salad as a Main Course

Salads for Health and Wellness

- The Mediterranean Diet and Health Benefits
- Weight Management with Mediterranean Salads
- Dietary Restrictions and Adaptations

Kids and Family-Friendly Salads

- Getting Kids to Love Veggies
- Fun and Creative Salad Ideas
- Family Mealtime Traditions

Mediterranean Salad Challenges

- Troubleshooting Tips
- Handling Leftovers
- Storing Salad Ingredients

Conclusion and Beyond

- Mediterranean Salad Revolution
- Your Journey Continues

Chapter 1: Introduction to Mediterranean Salads

The Mediterranean Diet: A Healthy Way of Life

The Mediterranean region has long been celebrated for its bountiful harvests, robust flavors, and the remarkable health of its people. At the heart of this culinary tradition lies the Mediterranean diet, a way of eating that promotes wellness, longevity, and a deep appreciation for fresh, whole foods. And at the forefront of this diet are the vibrant and diverse Mediterranean salads.

The Mediterranean Diet Essentials

The Mediterranean diet is not just about what you eat; it's a lifestyle that encompasses a love for good food, leisurely meals, and connection with family and friends. It's a diet that emphasizes the following key principles:

1. Abundant Fresh Produce

Mediterranean cuisine is renowned for its generous use of fresh fruits and vegetables. The abundance of colorful produce provides essential vitamins, minerals, and antioxidants that support overall health.

2. Heart-Healthy Fats

Olive oil, often referred to as "liquid gold," is a staple in Mediterranean cooking. Its monounsaturated fats are associated with reduced risk of heart disease and inflammation.

3. Lean Protein Sources

Fish and poultry are favored over red meat, providing a lean source of protein. Fatty fish like salmon and sardines supply omega-3 fatty acids, promoting heart health.

4. Whole Grains

Whole grains such as bulgur, couscous, and farro are commonly used, offering fiber and sustained energy.

5. Flavorful Herbs and Spices

Herbs like basil, oregano, and thyme, as well as spices like cumin and coriander, lend robust flavor without the need for excessive salt.

6. Moderate Wine Consumption

In moderation, red wine can be part of a Mediterranean meal, providing antioxidants like resveratrol, which may benefit heart health.

The Beauty of Mediterranean Salads

Mediterranean salads epitomize the principles of the Mediterranean diet. They are not just side dishes but often the centerpiece of a meal, bursting with flavors, colors, and textures. Here's what makes Mediterranean salads so special:

1. Versatile Ingredients

Mediterranean salads celebrate an array of ingredients, from ripe tomatoes and crisp cucumbers to creamy feta cheese and plump olives. The possibilities are as diverse as the region itself.

2. Balanced Nutrition

These salads offer a perfect balance of macronutrients - carbohydrates, proteins, and healthy fats - making them satisfying and nourishing.

3. Adaptability

Mediterranean salads can be adapted to various dietary preferences and restrictions. Whether you're a vegetarian, vegan, or a meat lover, there's a Mediterranean salad for you.

4. Endless Creativity

The art of Mediterranean salad-making lies in your creativity. You can mix and match ingredients, experiment with dressings, and create salads to suit any occasion or mood.

In the chapters that follow, we'll explore the rich tapestry of Mediterranean salads, from classic Greek varieties to inventive creations inspired by the flavors of Italy, Spain, the Middle East, and beyond. You'll learn how to select the finest ingredients, master the art of salad dressing, and even delve into the world of Mediterranean salad bowls, all while embracing the healthful and joyful Mediterranean way of life.

So, let's embark on this culinary journey together as we discover the fresh and flavorful world of Mediterranean salads. It's a journey that promises not only delicious meals but also a healthier and happier you. Bon appétit!

Chapter 2: Essential Ingredients

In the vibrant world of Mediterranean salads, three key categories of ingredients stand out as the foundation of flavor, nutrition, and authenticity. From the rich, golden elixir of olive oil to the aromatic herbs and spices that infuse every bite, these essential ingredients are what make Mediterranean salads truly exceptional.

Olive Oil: Liquid Gold of the Mediterranean

Olive oil is more than just a cooking staple in Mediterranean cuisine; it's an emblem of the region's culinary heritage. Often referred to as "liquid gold," this luscious oil is extracted from the fruit of the olive tree and has been cherished for centuries. Here's why it's so integral to Mediterranean salads and cooking:

Flavor and Aroma

Olive oil is prized for its rich, fruity flavor and distinctive aroma. It serves as both a cooking medium and a finishing touch, adding depth and complexity to your salads.

Health Benefits

Rich in monounsaturated fats and antioxidants, olive oil is known to support heart health, reduce inflammation, and contribute to overall well-being.

Types of Olive Oil

Extra Virgin Olive Oil: This is the highest quality olive oil, extracted without the use of heat or chemicals. It has a robust flavor and is best used in dressings and for drizzling over salads just before serving.

Virgin Olive Oil: Slightly lower in quality than extra virgin, it's still a fine choice for salad dressings and cooking.

Pure Olive Oil: A blend of virgin and refined olive oils, this type is suitable for high-heat cooking but lacks the nuanced flavors of extra virgin.

Light Olive Oil: This refers to a refined olive oil with a milder flavor, often used in baking or frying.

Tips for Choosing Olive Oil

1. Look for bottles labeled "cold-pressed" or "first cold-pressed" to ensure the highest quality.
2. Choose olive oils with a harvest date to ensure freshness.
3. Experiment with different varieties and regions for unique flavor profiles.

Vinegars, Herbs, and Spices

The allure of Mediterranean salads comes from the artful combination of tartness, freshness, and depth of flavor. Vinegars, herbs, and spices play a pivotal role in achieving this balance.

Vinegars

Balsamic Vinegar: With its sweet and tangy notes, balsamic vinegar is a favorite for Mediterranean salads. Aged varieties offer a rich, syrupy consistency.

Red Wine Vinegar: Known for its sharp acidity and fruity undertones, red wine vinegar adds zing to dressings.

White Wine Vinegar: This vinegar is milder in flavor than red wine vinegar and pairs well with delicate greens.

Apple Cider Vinegar: Its slightly fruity and acidic profile complements a wide range of salad ingredients.

Lemon Juice: Freshly squeezed lemon juice adds a burst of citrusy brightness to salads.

Herbs and Spices

Mediterranean salads are a symphony of herbs and spices that elevate each bite. Some essential ones include:

Basil: Fragrant and sweet, basil pairs beautifully with tomatoes and mozzarella in Caprese salads.

Oregano: A staple in Greek and Italian cuisines, oregano lends a earthy, aromatic note.

Mint: Refreshing and aromatic, mint adds a burst of flavor to tabbouleh and fruit salads.

Cumin: Earthy and warm, cumin is a key spice in Middle Eastern salads.

Paprika: Smoky or sweet, paprika adds color and depth to dressings and garnishes.

Fresh Produce: The Heart of Mediterranean Salads

At the core of every Mediterranean salad are fresh, vibrant fruits and vegetables. The Mediterranean climate is conducive to growing a wide array of produce, and the cuisine makes the most of this bounty.

Tomatoes

Tomatoes are a Mediterranean salad staple, providing juiciness and a burst of color. Varieties like Roma, heirloom, and cherry tomatoes are often used.

Cucumbers

Crisp and hydrating, cucumbers add a refreshing crunch to salads. English cucumbers, with their thin skin, are a popular choice.

Bell Peppers

Red, yellow, and green bell peppers contribute sweetness and vibrant colors to your salad creations.

Red Onions

Sliced thinly or pickled, red onions offer a sharp, pungent flavor that balances the sweetness of other ingredients.

Greens

Leafy greens like romaine, arugula, and spinach provide a bed for your salad creations. They offer a variety of textures and flavors.

Olives

A hallmark of Mediterranean cuisine, olives come in various shapes, sizes, and flavors, from briny Kalamata to buttery Castelvetrano.

Feta Cheese

Creamy and tangy, feta cheese is a beloved addition to Greek and Mediterranean salads.

Artichoke Hearts

Tender and slightly nutty, artichoke hearts add a unique texture and flavor to salads.

Avocado

Creamy and rich, avocado adds healthy fats and a luxurious mouthfeel.

Fresh Herbs

Fresh herbs like parsley, cilantro, and dill provide bursts of flavor and vibrant color.

In the chapters that follow, you'll discover how to combine these essential ingredients to create a wide range of Mediterranean salads, each with its own unique personality and flavor profile. As you become more acquainted with these ingredients, you'll gain the confidence to experiment, adapt, and create your own salad masterpieces.

Chapter 3: Classic Greek Salads

Traditional Greek Salad (Horiatiki)

When one thinks of Mediterranean salads, the Traditional Greek Salad, or Horiatiki, is often the first that comes to mind. With its vibrant colors, bold flavors, and a delightful combination of fresh ingredients, this salad is a true representation of the Mediterranean way of life.

Ingredients:

- 4 large ripe tomatoes, cut into wedges
- 1 cucumber, thinly sliced
- 1 red onion, thinly sliced
- 1 green bell pepper, thinly sliced
- 1 cup Kalamata olives, pitted
- 200g (7 oz) feta cheese, cubed or crumbled
- Fresh oregano leaves for garnish
- Extra virgin olive oil
- Red wine vinegar
- Salt and freshly ground black pepper to taste

Instructions:

1. In a large salad bowl, combine the tomato wedges, cucumber slices, red onion, and green bell pepper.
2. Add the Kalamata olives and cubed or crumbled feta cheese on top.
3. Drizzle extra virgin olive oil and red wine vinegar over the salad. The quantities can vary depending on your preference for dressing, but a good rule of thumb is a 3:1 ratio of olive oil to vinegar.
4. Season with salt and freshly ground black pepper to taste.
5. Gently toss all the ingredients together, being careful not to

crush the feta cheese.

6. Garnish with fresh oregano leaves.
7. Serve immediately as an appetizer or side dish with crusty bread to soak up the delicious juices.

Note: Traditional Greek Salad is versatile and open to personalization. You can add or omit ingredients based on your preferences, but the key is to showcase the freshness of the produce and the quality of the olive oil and feta cheese.

Greek Pasta Salad with Feta

This Greek Pasta Salad is a delightful twist on the classic. It combines the beloved flavors of Greek cuisine with the heartiness of pasta, making it a perfect option for picnics and potlucks.

Ingredients:

- 250g (9 oz) fusilli or rotini pasta, cooked and cooled
- 1 cup cherry tomatoes, halved
- 1/2 cup cucumber, diced
- 1/2 cup red bell pepper, diced
- 1/2 cup red onion, finely chopped
- 1/2 cup Kalamata olives, pitted and sliced
- 200g (7 oz) feta cheese, cubed or crumbled
- Fresh parsley leaves for garnish
- Extra virgin olive oil
- Red wine vinegar
- Salt and freshly ground black pepper to taste

Instructions:

1. In a large mixing bowl, combine the cooked and cooled pasta with the cherry tomatoes, cucumber, red bell pepper, red onion, Kalamata olives, and feta cheese.
2. Drizzle extra virgin olive oil and red wine vinegar over the salad. Again, use a 3:1 ratio of olive oil to vinegar.
3. Season with salt and freshly ground black pepper to taste.
4. Gently toss all the ingredients until well combined.
5. Garnish with fresh parsley leaves.
6. Refrigerate the salad for at least an hour before serving to allow the flavors to meld together.
7. Serve as a standalone dish or as a side at your next gathering.

Greek Couscous Salad

Couscous, a staple in Mediterranean cuisine, forms the base of this Greek-inspired salad. It's light, refreshing, and perfect for warm summer days.

Ingredients:

- 1 cup couscous
- 1 1/2 cups boiling water or vegetable broth
- 1 cup cherry tomatoes, halved
- 1/2 cup cucumber, diced
- 1/2 cup red onion, finely chopped
- 1/2 cup Kalamata olives, pitted and sliced
- 200g (7 oz) feta cheese, cubed or crumbled
- Fresh mint leaves for garnish
- Extra virgin olive oil
- Lemon juice
- Salt and freshly ground black pepper to taste

Instructions:

1. Place the couscous in a large heatproof bowl and pour the boiling water or vegetable broth over it. Cover the bowl with a lid or plastic wrap and let it sit for about 5 minutes or until the liquid is absorbed.
2. Fluff the couscous with a fork and allow it to cool completely.
3. In a separate mixing bowl, combine the cooled couscous with the cherry tomatoes, cucumber, red onion, Kalamata olives, and feta cheese.
4. Drizzle extra virgin olive oil and lemon juice over the salad, adjusting the quantities to your taste.
5. Season with salt and freshly ground black pepper.
6. Gently toss the ingredients together until well combined.
7. Garnish with fresh mint leaves.

8. Serve this delightful Greek Couscous Salad as a light and satisfying meal on its own or as a side dish for grilled meats and seafood.

These classic Greek salads showcase the Mediterranean tradition of using fresh, high-quality ingredients to create dishes that are not only delicious but also nutritious.

Chapter 4: Italian Delights

Caprese Salad: Tomatoes and Mozzarella

The Caprese Salad is a masterpiece of simplicity, allowing the quality of its ingredients to shine. With ripe tomatoes, fresh mozzarella, fragrant basil, and a drizzle of olive oil, it's a classic Italian salad that celebrates the essence of Mediterranean cuisine.

Ingredients:

- 4 large ripe tomatoes, sliced
- 200g (7 oz) fresh mozzarella cheese, sliced
- Fresh basil leaves
- Extra virgin olive oil
- Balsamic vinegar (optional)
- Salt and freshly ground black pepper to taste

Instructions:

1. Arrange the tomato and mozzarella slices on a serving platter, alternating them.
2. Tuck fresh basil leaves between the tomato and mozzarella slices.
3. Drizzle extra virgin olive oil generously over the salad. If desired, add a few drops of balsamic vinegar for extra flavor.
4. Season with salt and freshly ground black pepper to taste.
5. Serve the Caprese Salad as an appetizer or a light, refreshing side dish, especially during the summer months when tomatoes and basil are at their peak.

Panzanella: Tuscan Bread Salad

Panzanella is a Tuscan specialty that transforms stale bread into a delightful salad. It's a perfect example of Italian resourcefulness and a celebration of rustic flavors.

Ingredients:

- 4 cups stale Italian or rustic bread, torn into bite-sized pieces
- 4 ripe tomatoes, cut into chunks
- 1 cucumber, sliced
- 1 red onion, thinly sliced
- 1/2 cup Kalamata olives, pitted
- Fresh basil leaves
- Extra virgin olive oil
- Red wine vinegar
- Salt and freshly ground black pepper to taste

Instructions:

1. Place the torn bread in a large salad bowl.
2. Add the tomato chunks, cucumber slices, red onion, and Kalamata olives.
3. Tear fresh basil leaves and add them to the salad.
4. Drizzle extra virgin olive oil and red wine vinegar over the salad. Use a 3:1 ratio of olive oil to vinegar, adjusting to taste.
5. Season with salt and freshly ground black pepper.
6. Gently toss the salad to combine all the ingredients.
7. Allow the Panzanella to sit for about 20-30 minutes before serving, allowing the bread to soak up the flavors and juices.
8. Serve this Tuscan Bread Salad as a hearty appetizer or as a side dish with grilled meats and fish.

Insalata di Riso: Italian Rice Salad

Insalata di Riso, or Italian Rice Salad, is a cool and refreshing dish that's perfect for picnics and gatherings. It combines tender rice with colorful vegetables and a zesty dressing.

Ingredients:

- 1 1/2 cups Arborio rice, cooked and cooled

- 1/2 cup cherry tomatoes, halved
- 1/2 cup red bell pepper, diced
- 1/2 cup green bell pepper, diced
- 1/2 cup frozen peas, thawed
- 1/2 cup black olives, sliced
- 1/2 cup canned corn kernels, drained
- 1/4 cup fresh parsley, chopped
- 200g (7 oz) mozzarella cheese, cubed
- Extra virgin olive oil
- Red wine vinegar
- Dijon mustard
- Salt and freshly ground black pepper to taste

Instructions:

1. In a large mixing bowl, combine the cooked and cooled Arborio rice with the cherry tomatoes, red bell pepper, green bell pepper, peas, black olives, corn kernels, parsley, and mozzarella cheese.
2. In a separate small bowl, whisk together extra virgin olive oil, red wine vinegar, and a touch of Dijon mustard. Use a 3:1 ratio of olive oil to vinegar, adjusting to your taste.
3. Season the dressing with salt and freshly ground black pepper.
4. Drizzle the dressing over the rice and vegetable mixture.
5. Gently toss all the ingredients together until well coated with the dressing.
6. Refrigerate the Insalata di Riso for at least an hour before serving, allowing the flavors to meld together.
7. Serve this Italian Rice Salad as a refreshing side dish or a light meal on its own.

These Italian salads capture the essence of Italian cuisine, from the simplicity of the Caprese Salad to the rustic charm of Panzanella and the refreshing allure of Insalata di Riso. Each dish is a delicious ode to the Mediterranean's culinary diversity and the Italian art of savoring life's simple pleasures.

Chapter 5: Spanish Sensations

Gazpacho Salad

Gazpacho is a beloved Spanish cold tomato soup, and this Gazpacho Salad takes its refreshing flavors and transforms them into a delightful salad. It's perfect for those hot summer days when you crave something light and cool.

Ingredients:

- 4 large ripe tomatoes, diced
- 1 cucumber, diced
- 1 red bell pepper, diced
- 1 small red onion, finely chopped
- 2 cloves garlic, minced
- 1/4 cup fresh basil leaves, chopped
- 1/4 cup fresh parsley leaves, chopped
- 4 cups tomato juice
- 1/4 cup red wine vinegar
- 1/4 cup extra virgin olive oil
- Salt and freshly ground black pepper to taste

Instructions:

1. In a large salad bowl, combine the diced tomatoes, cucumber, red bell pepper, red onion, minced garlic, fresh basil, and fresh parsley.
2. In a separate pitcher, mix together the tomato juice, red wine vinegar, and extra virgin olive oil.
3. Pour the tomato juice mixture over the salad.
4. Season with salt and freshly ground black pepper to taste.
5. Gently toss all the ingredients together until well combined.
6. Refrigerate the Gazpacho Salad for at least an hour before

serving, allowing the flavors to meld and the salad to chill.

7. Serve this refreshing Spanish salad as a starter or a light meal, and garnish with additional basil and parsley if desired.

Ensalada Mixta: Mixed Spanish Salad

Ensalada Mixta, or Mixed Spanish Salad, is a colorful and satisfying dish that showcases the variety of fresh produce available in Spain. It's often served as a tapa or a side dish.

Ingredients:

- 4 cups mixed salad greens (lettuce, arugula, spinach)
- 2 ripe tomatoes, sliced
- 1/2 cucumber, sliced
- 1/2 red onion, thinly sliced
- 1 can (6 oz) tuna in olive oil, drained
- 2 hard-boiled eggs, sliced
- 1/4 cup pitted green olives
- 1/4 cup pitted black olives
- 4-6 anchovy fillets (optional)
- Extra virgin olive oil
- Red wine vinegar
- Salt and freshly ground black pepper to taste

Instructions:

1. Arrange the mixed salad greens on a serving platter.
2. Top the greens with sliced tomatoes, cucumber, and red onion.
3. Scatter the drained tuna over the salad.
4. Add the sliced hard-boiled eggs and both green and black olives.
5. If using anchovy fillets, arrange them on top.
6. Drizzle extra virgin olive oil and red wine vinegar over the salad, adjusting to your taste.
7. Season with salt and freshly ground black pepper.
8. Serve this vibrant Mixed Spanish Salad as a tapa or a side dish, ideally with a slice of crusty bread to soak up the dressing.

Salmorejo: Creamy Tomato and Bread Soup Salad

Salmorejo is a traditional Spanish tomato and bread soup from the Andalusian region. This salad adaptation retains the soup's creamy essence while offering a unique salad experience.

Ingredients:

- 4 large ripe tomatoes, diced
- 2 cloves garlic, minced
- 2 cups day-old bread, torn into pieces
- 1/4 cup extra virgin olive oil
- 2 tablespoons red wine vinegar
- 1/2 teaspoon salt
- Hard-boiled eggs and jamón serrano (Spanish ham) for garnish (optional)

Instructions:

1. In a blender or food processor, combine the diced tomatoes, minced garlic, torn bread, extra virgin olive oil, red wine vinegar, and salt.
2. Blend until the mixture is smooth and creamy.
3. If the mixture is too thick, you can add a bit of water to achieve the desired consistency.
4. Refrigerate the Salmorejo mixture for at least an hour to chill and allow the flavors to meld.
5. To serve, divide the Salmorejo mixture into individual bowls or glasses.
6. Garnish with slices of hard-boiled eggs and bits of jamón serrano, if desired.

This Creamy Tomato and Bread Soup Salad can be served as a chilled appetizer or a unique side dish.

These Spanish-inspired salads offer a taste of the Iberian Peninsula's diverse and flavorful cuisine. From the cool and refreshing Gazpacho Salad to the hearty and colorful Ensalada Mixta and the creamy delight of Salmorejo, each salad showcases the essence of Spanish cuisine and is sure to please your palate.

Chapter 6: Middle Eastern Inspirations

Tabouleh: Fresh Herb and Bulgur Salad

Tabouleh is a classic Middle Eastern salad known for its vibrant green colors and refreshing flavors. It's a delightful blend of fresh herbs, nutty bulgur, and zesty lemon, making it a perfect choice for those seeking a light and healthful salad.

Ingredients:

- 1 cup fine bulgur
- 1 1/2 cups boiling water
- 2 cups fresh parsley, finely chopped
- 1 cup fresh mint leaves, finely chopped
- 4 ripe tomatoes, diced
- 2 green onions, finely chopped
- Juice of 2 lemons
- 1/4 cup extra virgin olive oil
- Salt and freshly ground black pepper to taste

Instructions:

1. Place the fine bulgur in a heatproof bowl, and pour the boiling water over it. Cover the bowl with a lid or plastic wrap and let it sit for about 20 minutes, or until the bulgur absorbs the water and becomes tender.
2. Fluff the cooked bulgur with a fork and allow it to cool completely.
3. In a large salad bowl, combine the cooled bulgur, chopped fresh parsley, fresh mint leaves, diced tomatoes, and finely chopped green onions.
4. In a separate small bowl, whisk together the lemon juice and extra virgin olive oil.

5. Pour the lemon juice and olive oil dressing over the salad.

6. Season with salt and freshly ground black pepper to taste.

7. Gently toss all the ingredients together until well combined.

8. Refrigerate the Tabouleh for about an hour before serving, allowing the flavors to meld and the salad to chill.

9. Serve this Fresh Herb and Bulgur Salad as a side dish or a light meal. It's especially delicious wrapped in lettuce leaves.

Fattoush: Lebanese Bread Salad

Fattoush is a Lebanese bread salad that showcases the wonderful practice of using stale bread creatively. With its combination of crispy pita, fresh vegetables, and zesty dressing, it's a Middle Eastern culinary gem.

Ingredients:

- 2 large pita bread rounds, toasted and broken into pieces
- 2 cups cucumber, diced
- 2 cups tomatoes, diced
- 1 cup red bell pepper, diced
- 1 cup red onion, thinly sliced
- 1/2 cup fresh parsley leaves, chopped
- 1/4 cup fresh mint leaves, chopped
- 1/4 cup fresh cilantro leaves, chopped
- 1/4 cup extra virgin olive oil
- Juice of 2 lemons
- 1 teaspoon ground sumac (optional, for extra flavor)
- Salt and freshly ground black pepper to taste

Instructions:

1. Toast the pita bread rounds until they become crisp and golden. Break them into bite-sized pieces.
2. In a large salad bowl, combine the toasted pita pieces, diced cucumber, diced tomatoes, diced red bell pepper, thinly sliced red onion, chopped fresh parsley, chopped fresh mint leaves, and chopped fresh cilantro leaves.
3. In a separate small bowl, whisk together the extra virgin olive oil, lemon juice, ground sumac (if using), salt, and freshly ground black pepper.
4. Drizzle the dressing over the salad.
5. Gently toss all the ingredients together until the dressing evenly

coats the salad.

6. Let the Fattoush salad sit for about 10 minutes before serving, allowing the flavors to meld slightly and the pita to soften slightly.

7. Serve this Lebanese Bread Salad as a refreshing and satisfying side dish or a light meal.

Moroccan Chickpea and Couscous Salad

This Moroccan-inspired salad combines the flavors of North Africa with the healthful ingredients of the Mediterranean. It's a hearty and nutritious dish that's perfect for lunch or dinner.

Ingredients:

- 1 cup couscous
- 1 1/2 cups boiling water or vegetable broth
- 1 can (15 oz) chickpeas, drained and rinsed
- 1 cup cherry tomatoes, halved
- 1/2 cup cucumber, diced
- 1/2 cup red bell pepper, diced
- 1/2 cup red onion, finely chopped
- 1/4 cup fresh cilantro leaves, chopped
- 1/4 cup fresh parsley leaves, chopped
- 1/4 cup extra virgin olive oil
- Juice of 2 lemons
- 1 teaspoon ground cumin
- 1/2 teaspoon ground coriander
- Salt and freshly ground black pepper to taste

Instructions:

1. Place the couscous in a large heatproof bowl and pour the boiling water or vegetable broth over it. Cover the bowl with a lid or plastic wrap and let it sit for about 5 minutes or until the liquid is absorbed.
2. Fluff the couscous with a fork and allow it to cool completely.
3. In a large mixing bowl, combine the cooled couscous, drained and rinsed chickpeas, halved cherry tomatoes, diced cucumber, diced red bell pepper, finely chopped red onion, chopped fresh cilantro leaves, and chopped fresh parsley leaves.
4. In a separate small bowl, whisk together the extra virgin olive

oil, lemon juice, ground cumin, ground coriander, salt, and freshly ground black pepper.

5. Pour the dressing over the salad.
6. Gently toss all the ingredients together until well combined.
7. Refrigerate the Moroccan Chickpea and Couscous Salad for at least an hour before serving, allowing the flavors to meld.
8. Serve this hearty salad as a standalone dish or as a side to grilled meats or fish.

These Middle Eastern-inspired salads bring the exotic flavors of the Mediterranean and North Africa to your table. From the refreshing Tabouleh and crispy Fattoush to the hearty Moroccan Chickpea and Couscous Salad, each dish is a celebration of bold and aromatic ingredients.

Chapter 7: Mediterranean Protein-Packed Salads

Tuna Niçoise Salad

The Tuna Niçoise Salad is a French-inspired classic that has become a Mediterranean favorite. It combines tender tuna, crisp vegetables, and briny olives into a satisfying and protein-rich salad.

Ingredients:

- 2 cans (5 oz each) tuna, drained
- 4 cups mixed salad greens (lettuce, arugula, spinach)
- 4 hard-boiled eggs, halved
- 1 cup cherry tomatoes, halved
- 1/2 cup green beans, blanched and cut into bite-sized pieces
- 1/2 cup Niçoise olives
- 1/4 cup red onion, thinly sliced
- 2 tablespoons capers
- Lemon wedges for garnish
- Extra virgin olive oil
- Red wine vinegar
- Salt and freshly ground black pepper to taste

Instructions:

1. Arrange the mixed salad greens on a serving platter.
2. Top the greens with the drained tuna.
3. Surround the tuna with halved hard-boiled eggs, cherry tomatoes, blanched green beans, Niçoise olives, thinly sliced red onion, and capers.
4. Drizzle extra virgin olive oil and red wine vinegar over the salad, adjusting to your taste.
5. Season with salt and freshly ground black pepper.

6. Garnish with lemon wedges.
7. Serve this Tuna Niçoise Salad as a hearty and protein-packed meal.

Grilled Chicken and Quinoa Salad

This Grilled Chicken and Quinoa Salad is a satisfying and nutritious dish that combines the goodness of lean protein, whole grains, and fresh vegetables.

Ingredients:

- 2 boneless, skinless chicken breasts
- 1 cup quinoa, cooked and cooled
- 4 cups mixed salad greens (lettuce, arugula, spinach)
- 1 cup cherry tomatoes, halved
- 1/2 cup cucumber, diced
- 1/2 cup red bell pepper, diced
- 1/4 cup red onion, finely chopped
- 1/4 cup Kalamata olives, pitted and sliced
- 1/4 cup feta cheese, crumbled
- Extra virgin olive oil
- Balsamic vinegar
- Dijon mustard
- Salt and freshly ground black pepper to taste

Instructions:

1. Season the chicken breasts with salt and freshly ground black pepper. Grill or cook the chicken until it's cooked through and has grill marks, about 4-6 minutes per side. Let the chicken rest for a few minutes before slicing it.
2. In a large mixing bowl, combine the cooked and cooled quinoa, mixed salad greens, halved cherry tomatoes, diced cucumber, diced red bell pepper, finely chopped red onion, Kalamata olives, and crumbled feta cheese.
3. In a separate small bowl, whisk together extra virgin olive oil, balsamic vinegar, and a touch of Dijon mustard. Use a 3:1 ratio of olive oil to vinegar, adjusting to your taste.

4. Drizzle the dressing over the salad.
5. Gently toss all the ingredients together until well combined.
6. Top the salad with sliced grilled chicken.
7. Serve this Grilled Chicken and Quinoa Salad as a wholesome and protein-packed meal.

Lentil and Roasted Vegetable Salad

Lentils are a protein powerhouse, and when combined with roasted vegetables, they create a hearty and satisfying salad that's perfect for vegetarians and meat-lovers alike.

Ingredients:

- 1 cup green or brown lentils, rinsed and drained
- 4 cups mixed salad greens (lettuce, arugula, spinach)
- 2 cups assorted roasted vegetables (bell peppers, zucchini, eggplant, carrots, etc.)
- 1/2 cup cherry tomatoes, halved
- 1/4 cup red onion, thinly sliced
- 1/4 cup feta cheese, crumbled
- Extra virgin olive oil
- Balsamic vinegar
- Dijon mustard
- Salt and freshly ground black pepper to taste

Instructions:

1. In a medium saucepan, bring 2 1/2 cups of water to a boil. Add the lentils, reduce heat, and simmer for about 20-25 minutes, or until the lentils are tender but not mushy. Drain any excess water and let the lentils cool.
2. In a large mixing bowl, combine the cooked lentils, mixed salad greens, assorted roasted vegetables, halved cherry tomatoes, thinly sliced red onion, and crumbled feta cheese.
3. In a separate small bowl, whisk together extra virgin olive oil, balsamic vinegar, and a touch of Dijon mustard. Use a 3:1 ratio of olive oil to vinegar, adjusting to your taste.
4. Drizzle the dressing over the salad.
5. Gently toss all the ingredients together until well combined.
6. Serve this Lentil and Roasted Vegetable Salad as a hearty and

protein-packed meal.

These protein-packed Mediterranean salads are not only delicious but also nutritious, providing you with a satisfying and wholesome meal. Whether you prefer the classic flavors of Tuna Niçoise, the grilled goodness of Grilled Chicken and Quinoa, or the hearty simplicity of Lentil and Roasted Vegetable Salad, each dish brings its unique charm to your table.

Chapter 8: Refreshing Seafood Salads

Shrimp and Orzo Salad

This Shrimp and Orzo Salad is a delightful combination of tender shrimp, toothsome orzo pasta, and a medley of fresh vegetables. It's a refreshing and protein-rich salad that's perfect for seafood lovers.

Ingredients:

- 1 cup orzo pasta, cooked and cooled
- 1 pound large shrimp, peeled, deveined, and cooked
- 1 cup cherry tomatoes, halved
- 1/2 cup cucumber, diced
- 1/4 cup red onion, finely chopped
- 1/4 cup fresh parsley, chopped
- 1/4 cup fresh dill, chopped
- 1/4 cup feta cheese, crumbled
- Extra virgin olive oil
- Lemon juice
- Salt and freshly ground black pepper to taste

Instructions:

1. In a large mixing bowl, combine the cooked and cooled orzo pasta, cooked shrimp, halved cherry tomatoes, diced cucumber, finely chopped red onion, chopped fresh parsley, chopped fresh dill, and crumbled feta cheese.
2. Drizzle extra virgin olive oil and lemon juice over the salad, adjusting to your taste.
3. Season with salt and freshly ground black pepper.
4. Gently toss all the ingredients together until well combined.
5. Refrigerate the Shrimp and Orzo Salad for at least an hour before serving, allowing the flavors to meld.

6. Serve this seafood delight as a refreshing main course or a satisfying side dish.

Calamari Salad with Lemon and Herbs

Calamari salad is a Mediterranean favorite, known for its bright and zesty flavors. This version combines tender calamari with fresh herbs and a tangy lemon dressing.

Ingredients:

- 1 pound cleaned calamari, tubes and tentacles
- 2 tablespoons extra virgin olive oil
- Juice of 2 lemons
- 2 cloves garlic, minced
- 1/4 cup fresh parsley, chopped
- 1/4 cup fresh cilantro, chopped
- 1/4 cup fresh mint leaves, chopped
- 1/4 cup red onion, finely chopped
- Salt and freshly ground black pepper to taste
- Red pepper flakes (optional, for a bit of heat)

Instructions:

1. Bring a large pot of salted water to a boil. Add the cleaned calamari and cook for 1-2 minutes until just tender. Drain and rinse under cold water.
2. In a large mixing bowl, combine the cooked calamari with extra virgin olive oil, lemon juice, minced garlic, chopped fresh parsley, chopped fresh cilantro, chopped fresh mint leaves, and finely chopped red onion.
3. Season with salt and freshly ground black pepper. If desired, add a pinch of red pepper flakes for some heat.
4. Gently toss all the ingredients together until well combined.
5. Refrigerate the Calamari Salad for at least an hour before

serving, allowing the flavors to meld.

6. Serve this zesty and herbaceous salad as a refreshing appetizer or a light main course.

Mediterranean Octopus Salad

Mediterranean Octopus Salad is a true seafood delicacy. The tender octopus is paired with a flavorful dressing, creating a salad that's as impressive as it is delicious.

Ingredients:

- 2 pounds octopus, cleaned and cooked
- 1/2 cup red onion, thinly sliced
- 1/4 cup fresh parsley, chopped
- 1/4 cup fresh mint leaves, chopped
- 1/4 cup Kalamata olives, pitted and sliced
- Extra virgin olive oil
- Red wine vinegar
- Salt and freshly ground black pepper to taste
- Lemon wedges for garnish

Instructions:

1. Slice the cooked octopus into bite-sized pieces.
2. In a large mixing bowl, combine the sliced octopus, thinly sliced red onion, chopped fresh parsley, chopped fresh mint leaves, and sliced Kalamata olives.
3. Drizzle extra virgin olive oil and red wine vinegar over the salad, adjusting to your taste.
4. Season with salt and freshly ground black pepper.
5. Gently toss all the ingredients together until well combined.
6. Refrigerate the Mediterranean Octopus Salad for at least an hour before serving, allowing the flavors to meld.
7. Serve this elegant and flavorful salad as a show-stopping appetizer or a special main course, garnished with lemon wedges.

These refreshing seafood salads bring the taste of the Mediterranean sea to your plate. From the protein-packed Shrimp and Orzo Salad to the zesty Calamari Salad and the elegant Mediterranean Octopus Salad, each dish is a celebration of seafood's delicious versatility.

Chapter 9: Vegan and Vegetarian Creations

Mediterranean Chickpea Salad

Mediterranean Chickpea Salad is a vegan delight that brings together the earthy flavors of chickpeas with vibrant Mediterranean vegetables and herbs. It's a protein-rich and satisfying salad that's perfect for vegans and vegetarians.

Ingredients:

- 2 cans (15 oz each) chickpeas, drained and rinsed
- 1 cup cherry tomatoes, halved
- 1 cucumber, diced
- 1/2 cup red onion, finely chopped
- 1/4 cup fresh parsley, chopped
- 1/4 cup fresh mint leaves, chopped
- 1/4 cup Kalamata olives, pitted and sliced
- 1/4 cup extra virgin olive oil
- Juice of 2 lemons
- 2 cloves garlic, minced
- Salt and freshly ground black pepper to taste

Instructions:

In a large mixing bowl, combine the drained and rinsed chickpeas, halved cherry tomatoes, diced cucumber, finely chopped red onion, chopped fresh parsley, chopped fresh mint leaves, and sliced Kalamata olives.

In a separate small bowl, whisk together extra virgin olive oil, lemon juice, minced garlic, salt, and freshly ground black pepper.

Drizzle the dressing over the salad, adjusting to your taste.

Gently toss all the ingredients together until well combined.

Refrigerate the Mediterranean Chickpea Salad for at least an hour before serving, allowing the flavors to meld.

Serve this vegan and protein-packed salad as a standalone dish or as a side to your favorite Mediterranean meal.

Roasted Eggplant and Red Pepper Salad

Roasted Eggplant and Red Pepper Salad is a delicious and satisfying vegan salad that highlights the smoky flavors of roasted vegetables. It's a perfect blend of textures and tastes.

Ingredients:

- 2 medium eggplants, diced
- 2 red bell peppers, diced
- 1/4 cup red onion, finely chopped
- 1/4 cup fresh parsley, chopped
- 1/4 cup fresh cilantro, chopped
- 1/4 cup extra virgin olive oil
- Juice of 2 lemons
- 2 cloves garlic, minced
- Ground cumin, to taste
- Ground paprika, to taste
- Salt and freshly ground black pepper to taste

Instructions:

Preheat your oven to 425°F (220°C).

In a large mixing bowl, combine the diced eggplants and diced red bell peppers.

Drizzle extra virgin olive oil over the vegetables, then sprinkle with ground cumin, ground paprika, salt, and freshly ground black pepper. Toss to coat the vegetables evenly.

Spread the seasoned vegetables in a single layer on a baking sheet.

Roast in the preheated oven for about 25-30 minutes, or until the vegetables are tender and slightly charred.

Let the roasted vegetables cool to room temperature.

In a large salad bowl, combine the roasted eggplants and red bell peppers with finely chopped red onion, chopped fresh parsley, and chopped fresh cilantro.

In a separate small bowl, whisk together the lemon juice and minced garlic.

Drizzle the dressing over the salad, adjusting to your taste.

Gently toss all the ingredients together until well combined.

Serve this Roasted Eggplant and Red Pepper Salad as a flavorful and hearty vegan dish.

Spinach and Walnut Salad

Spinach and Walnut Salad is a simple yet satisfying vegan salad that combines the earthy flavors of spinach with the richness of walnuts. It's a nutritious and flavorful choice for vegans and vegetarians.

Ingredients:

- 4 cups fresh baby spinach leaves
- 1/2 cup walnuts, toasted and chopped
- 1/4 cup red onion, thinly sliced
- 1/4 cup dried cranberries or raisins
- 1/4 cup balsamic vinegar
- 1/4 cup extra virgin olive oil
- 1 tablespoon Dijon mustard
- Salt and freshly ground black pepper to taste

Instructions:

In a large salad bowl, combine the fresh baby spinach leaves, toasted and chopped walnuts, thinly sliced red onion, and dried cranberries or raisins.

In a separate small bowl, whisk together the balsamic vinegar, extra virgin olive oil, Dijon mustard, salt, and freshly ground black pepper.

Drizzle the dressing over the salad, adjusting to your taste.

Gently toss all the ingredients together until the spinach is coated with the dressing.

Serve this simple and satisfying Spinach and Walnut Salad as a nutritious vegan dish or a delightful side.

These vegan and vegetarian Mediterranean salads offer a burst of fresh flavors and plant-based goodness. Whether you prefer the protein-rich Mediterranean Chickpea Salad, the smoky Roasted Eggplant and Red Pepper Salad, or the simple yet satisfying Spinach and Walnut Salad, each dish is a testament to the delicious variety of vegan and vegetarian options available in Mediterranean cuisine.

Chapter 10: Inventive Salad Dressings

Lemon-Tahini Dressing

Lemon-Tahini Dressing is a creamy and zesty dressing that adds a burst of flavor to your salads. It's versatile and can be used to elevate a variety of Mediterranean-inspired salads.

Ingredients:

- 1/4 cup tahini (sesame paste)
- Juice of 2 lemons
- 2 cloves garlic, minced
- 2 tablespoons extra virgin olive oil
- 2 tablespoons water
- 1 teaspoon ground cumin
- Salt and freshly ground black pepper to taste

Instructions:

In a small bowl, combine tahini, lemon juice, minced garlic, extra virgin olive oil, water, ground cumin, salt, and freshly ground black pepper.

Whisk together until the ingredients are well blended and the dressing reaches a creamy consistency.

Taste and adjust the seasoning if needed by adding more lemon juice, salt, or pepper.

Drizzle the Lemon-Tahini Dressing over your favorite Mediterranean salads and toss to combine. It also works wonderfully as a dipping sauce for pita bread or vegetable sticks.

Pomegranate Vinaigrette

Pomegranate Vinaigrette is a sweet and tangy dressing that's bursting with fruity flavors. It adds a refreshing twist to your salads and pairs beautifully with fruits and nuts.

Ingredients:

- 1/2 cup pomegranate juice
- 1/4 cup extra virgin olive oil
- 2 tablespoons red wine vinegar
- 1 tablespoon honey or maple syrup (for a vegan version)
- 1 teaspoon Dijon mustard
- Salt and freshly ground black pepper to taste

Instructions:

In a small saucepan, bring the pomegranate juice to a simmer over low heat. Simmer for about 10-15 minutes, or until it reduces to about 1/4 cup. Let it cool.

In a mixing bowl, combine the reduced pomegranate juice, extra virgin olive oil, red wine vinegar, honey or maple syrup (for sweetness), Dijon mustard, salt, and freshly ground black pepper.

Whisk the ingredients together until the dressing is well emulsified.

Taste and adjust the sweetness or acidity as needed by adding more honey or vinegar.

Drizzle the Pomegranate Vinaigrette over your salads and enjoy the burst of fruity flavors. It's particularly delightful on salads with mixed greens, pomegranate seeds, and toasted nuts.

Honey Mustard Yogurt Dressing

Honey Mustard Yogurt Dressing is a creamy and slightly sweet dressing with a hint of tanginess. It's a healthier alternative to traditional creamy dressings and complements a wide range of salads.

Ingredients:

- 1/2 cup Greek yogurt (or any plain yogurt)
- 2 tablespoons Dijon mustard
- 2 tablespoons honey
- Juice of 1 lemon
- 2 tablespoons extra virgin olive oil
- Salt and freshly ground black pepper to taste

Instructions:

In a small mixing bowl, combine Greek yogurt, Dijon mustard, honey, lemon juice, extra virgin olive oil, salt, and freshly ground black pepper.

Whisk together until the ingredients are well combined and the dressing reaches a smooth and creamy consistency.

Taste and adjust the sweetness, acidity, or seasoning if needed by adding more honey, lemon juice, or salt.

Drizzle the Honey Mustard Yogurt Dressing over your salads for a creamy and slightly sweet flavor profile. It pairs wonderfully with salads featuring roasted vegetables, grilled chicken, or fruits.

These inventive salad dressings are the perfect finishing touch to elevate your Mediterranean salads to new heights of flavor. Whether you choose the creamy and zesty Lemon-Tahini Dressing, the sweet and tangy Pomegranate Vinaigrette, or the healthier Honey Mustard Yogurt Dressing, each one adds a unique twist to your salad creations.

Chapter 11: Salads for All Seasons

Summer Watermelon and Feta Salad

Summer Watermelon and Feta Salad is a refreshing and vibrant dish that celebrates the flavors of the season. It's a delightful combination of sweet watermelon, creamy feta cheese, and fresh herbs.

Ingredients:

- 4 cups cubed watermelon
- 1 cup feta cheese, crumbled
- 1/4 cup fresh mint leaves, chopped
- 1/4 cup fresh basil leaves, chopped
- 1/4 cup red onion, thinly sliced
- Extra virgin olive oil
- Balsamic glaze (optional)
- Salt and freshly ground black pepper to taste

Instructions:

1. In a large salad bowl, combine the cubed watermelon, crumbled feta cheese, chopped fresh mint leaves, chopped fresh basil leaves, and thinly sliced red onion.
2. Drizzle extra virgin olive oil over the salad, adjusting to your taste.
3. Season with salt and freshly ground black pepper.
4. Gently toss all the ingredients together until well combined.

1. If desired, drizzle with a balsamic glaze for an extra burst of flavor.
2. Serve this Summer Watermelon and Feta Salad as a refreshing side dish or a light summer meal.

Autumn Harvest Salad

Autumn Harvest Salad celebrates the rich and earthy flavors of the season. It combines roasted root vegetables, hearty grains, and seasonal fruits to create a satisfying and flavorful salad.

Ingredients:

- 2 cups mixed salad greens (lettuce, arugula, spinach)
- 2 cups roasted root vegetables (e.g., sweet potatoes, carrots, beets)
- 1 cup cooked quinoa, cooled
- 1 apple, thinly sliced
- 1/2 cup dried cranberries
- 1/2 cup chopped pecans, toasted
- Extra virgin olive oil
- Balsamic vinegar
- Dijon mustard
- Salt and freshly ground black pepper to taste

Instructions:

1. In a large salad bowl, combine the mixed salad greens, roasted root vegetables, cooked quinoa, thinly sliced apple, dried cranberries, and toasted chopped pecans.
2. In a separate small bowl, whisk together extra virgin olive oil, balsamic vinegar, a touch of Dijon mustard, salt, and freshly ground black pepper.
3. Drizzle the dressing over the salad, adjusting to your taste.
4. Gently toss all the ingredients together until well combined.
5. Serve this Autumn Harvest Salad as a hearty and flavorful dish that captures the essence of fall.

Winter Citrus Salad

Winter Citrus Salad brightens up the colder months with a burst of fresh and zesty citrus fruits. It's a colorful and vitamin-packed salad that's perfect for brightening your winter days.

Ingredients:

- 2 oranges, peeled and sliced into rounds
- 2 grapefruits, peeled and segmented
- 1 blood orange, peeled and sliced into rounds
- 1 fennel bulb, thinly sliced
- 1/4 red onion, thinly sliced
- 1/4 cup fresh mint leaves, chopped
- 1/4 cup pomegranate seeds
- Extra virgin olive oil
- Lemon juice
- Honey (optional, for sweetness)
- Salt and freshly ground black pepper to taste

Instructions:

1. Arrange the citrus slices on a serving platter.
2. Scatter the thinly sliced fennel, thinly sliced red onion, chopped fresh mint leaves, and pomegranate seeds over the citrus slices.
3. Drizzle extra virgin olive oil and lemon juice over the salad, adjusting to your taste. If desired, add a touch of honey for sweetness.
4. Season with salt and freshly ground black pepper.
5. Serve this Winter Citrus Salad as a vibrant and vitamin-rich addition to your winter menu.

These salads for all seasons embrace the unique flavors and ingredients of each time of year. Whether you choose the refreshing Summer Watermelon and Feta Salad, the hearty Autumn Harvest Salad, or the zesty Winter Citrus Salad, each dish is designed to complement the seasonal bounty and brighten your plate.

Chapter 12: Salad Presentation and Garnishes

Artful Plating

Artful Plating is the creative process of arranging your Mediterranean salads in a visually appealing manner. With a few tips and tricks, you can transform your salads into stunning works of culinary art.

Tips for Artful Plating:

Color Contrast: Use a variety of colorful ingredients to create contrast and vibrancy in your salad. Mix greens with reds, oranges, yellows, and purples to make the salad visually striking.

Layering: Build your salad in layers, placing the most vibrant and visually appealing ingredients on top. This adds depth and intrigue to your dish.

Shapes and Textures: Incorporate different shapes and textures, such as sliced vegetables, diced fruits, and crisp greens. Play with different cuts and arrangements to make your salad visually engaging.

Balance and Proportion: Pay attention to the balance and proportion of ingredients on the plate. Create harmony by distributing elements evenly and avoiding overcrowding.

Garnishes: Use edible garnishes like fresh herbs, microgreens, or edible flowers to add a pop of color and elegance to your dish.

Sauces and Drizzles: Consider drizzling dressings or sauces in artistic patterns over the salad. A well-executed drizzle can elevate the overall presentation.

Plate Choice: Choose the right plate or platter for your salad. The shape and color of the plate can complement the colors and arrangement of the salad.

Negative Space: Embrace negative space on the plate to allow your salad to breathe and to create a sense of balance.

Remember, artful plating is not just about aesthetics; it can enhance the dining experience and make your Mediterranean salads even more appealing.

Edible Flowers and Herbs

Edible flowers and herbs are not just for decoration; they add unique flavors, aromas, and a touch of elegance to your Mediterranean salads. Here are some options to consider:

Edible Flowers:

Nasturtium: These vibrant orange and yellow flowers have a peppery flavor, adding a delightful bite to salads.

Pansies: Pansies come in a variety of colors and have a mild, slightly grassy flavor that complements fresh greens.

Borage: Borage flowers are blue and have a subtle cucumber-like taste, making them a refreshing addition to salads.

Lavender: A few dried lavender buds can infuse your salad with a fragrant and floral note. Use sparingly.

Marigold: Marigold petals add a pop of color and a mildly spicy flavor to your salads.

Edible Herbs:

Basil: Fresh basil leaves are a classic addition to Mediterranean salads, offering a sweet and aromatic flavor.

Mint: Mint leaves provide a cool and refreshing contrast to other salad ingredients.

Parsley: Parsley adds a burst of freshness and green color to salads. Both flat-leaf and curly varieties work well.

Cilantro: Cilantro leaves have a citrusy, herbaceous flavor that can elevate your salad's taste.

Dill: Dill fronds bring a delicate anise-like flavor to your Mediterranean salads.

Experiment with these edible flowers and herbs to discover the flavor combinations that suit your taste and enhance the visual appeal of your salads.

Nut and Seed Crunch

Adding a nut and seed crunch to your salads not only provides a satisfying textural contrast but also boosts flavor and nutrition. Here are some options to consider:

Nuts:

Walnuts: Toasted walnuts add a rich, earthy flavor and a pleasant crunch to salads.

Almonds: Sliced or slivered almonds provide a nutty aroma and a subtle sweetness.

Pecans: Pecans have a buttery taste that complements a wide range of salad ingredients.

Pine Nuts: Toasted pine nuts offer a delicate, buttery flavor and a slight crunch.

Seeds:

Sunflower Seeds: Sunflower seeds are mild and nutty, adding a delightful crunch to salads.

Pumpkin Seeds (Pepitas): Pepitas have a slightly sweet and earthy flavor, perfect for Mediterranean salads.

Sesame Seeds: Toasted sesame seeds bring a nutty and aromatic quality to your dishes.

Chia Seeds: Chia seeds provide a gel-like texture when soaked, adding both crunch and nutrition.

Before adding nuts and seeds to your salad, it's a good practice to toast them briefly to enhance their flavor. Simply place them in a dry skillet over medium heat and stir until they become fragrant and lightly browned.

By incorporating these crunchy elements, you'll create a satisfying and dynamic salad experience that's both tasty and texturally pleasing.

Chapter 13: Mediterranean Salad Bowls

Building the Perfect Salad Bowl

Creating the perfect Mediterranean Salad Bowl is all about balance and variety. Follow these steps to build a satisfying and wholesome salad bowl:

1. Choose a Base:

Greens: Start with a bed of fresh greens like mixed lettuce, arugula, spinach, or kale. Greens provide the foundation of your salad bowl.

Grains: Consider adding cooked grains like quinoa, bulgur, couscous, or farro for added texture and heartiness.

2. Add Protein:

Protein: Include a source of protein like grilled chicken, shrimp, tofu, chickpeas, or beans to make your salad bowl more filling and nutritious.

3. Load Up on Vegetables:

Roasted Vegetables: Roasted or grilled vegetables like bell peppers, zucchini, eggplant, and carrots bring depth of flavor and color.

Fresh Vegetables: Add fresh and crisp veggies such as cucumbers, tomatoes, red onion, and cherry tomatoes for a burst of freshness.

4. Incorporate Fruits:

Fruits: Elevate your salad bowl with fruits like sliced strawberries, pomegranate seeds, or orange segments for a touch of sweetness and acidity.

5. Include Healthy Fats:

Healthy Fats: Enhance the creaminess and richness of your salad bowl with ingredients like avocado slices, olives, or a sprinkle of nuts and seeds.

6. Dress It Up:

Dressing: Drizzle your favorite Mediterranean-inspired dressing over the bowl. Options like Lemon-Tahini, Pomegranate Vinaigrette, or Balsamic Olive Oil work well.

7. Garnish:

Fresh Herbs: Finish your salad bowl with chopped fresh herbs like mint, basil, or parsley for a burst of flavor.

Crumbled Cheese: If you desire, crumble some feta or goat cheese on top for added creaminess and saltiness.

8. Season and Serve:

Seasoning: Season with salt and freshly ground black pepper to taste. You can also add a dash of lemon juice or extra virgin olive oil for extra flavor.

Once your Mediterranean Salad Bowl is assembled, toss gently to combine the ingredients evenly and enjoy a wholesome and balanced meal.

Breakfast Salad Bowl

A Breakfast Salad Bowl is a fresh and nutritious way to start your day. It combines the flavors of Mediterranean breakfast staples for a satisfying morning meal.

Ingredients:

- Base: Mixed greens or spinach
- Protein: Scrambled eggs or tofu scramble
- Vegetables: Sliced tomatoes, cucumbers, bell peppers, red onion
- Healthy Fats: Sliced avocado, Kalamata olives
- Dressing: Tzatziki sauce or yogurt-based dressing
- Fresh Herbs: Chopped fresh dill or parsley
- Optional Garnish: Crumbled feta cheese

Instructions:

1. Start with a bed of mixed greens or spinach in your bowl.
2. Add scrambled eggs or tofu scramble for protein.
3. Arrange sliced tomatoes, cucumbers, bell peppers, and red onion around the bowl.
4. Include sliced avocado and Kalamata olives for healthy fats.
5. Drizzle with tzatziki sauce or a yogurt-based dressing.

6. Garnish with chopped fresh dill or parsley and crumbled feta cheese if desired.

7. Season with salt and freshly ground black pepper to taste.

Enjoy your Breakfast Salad Bowl as a nutritious and refreshing morning meal.

Buddha Bowl

A Buddha Bowl is a well-balanced and vibrant meal that typically consists of a variety of plant-based ingredients. Here's a Mediterranean-inspired Buddha Bowl recipe:

Ingredients:

- Base: Cooked quinoa
- Protein: Roasted chickpeas (seasoned with Mediterranean spices)
- Roasted Vegetables: Cherry tomatoes, bell peppers, and red onion
- Fresh Vegetables: Sliced cucumber and baby spinach
- Healthy Fats: Sliced avocado and toasted pine nuts
- Dressing: Lemon-Tahini Dressing
- Garnish: Fresh mint leaves and pomegranate seeds

Instructions:

1. Start with a generous portion of cooked quinoa as the base of your Buddha Bowl.
2. Add roasted chickpeas for a protein-packed element.
3. Arrange roasted cherry tomatoes, bell peppers, and red onion for a burst of flavor.
4. Include sliced cucumber and baby spinach for freshness and crunch.
5. Top with sliced avocado and toasted pine nuts for healthy fats and a satisfying crunch.
6. Drizzle with Lemon-Tahini Dressing for creaminess and tang.
7. Garnish with fresh mint leaves and pomegranate seeds for a pop of color and flavor.
8. Season with salt and freshly ground black pepper to taste.

Enjoy your Mediterranean-inspired Buddha Bowl as a wholesome and balanced meal that's packed with flavor and nutrients.

Chapter 14: Salads for Special Occasions

Wedding and Celebration Salads

When it comes to weddings and special celebrations, salads can be both beautiful and delicious additions to your menu. Here are some elegant and celebratory Mediterranean salad ideas:

Caprese Skewers

Caprese Skewers are bite-sized bursts of Mediterranean flavor. These skewers feature cherry tomatoes, fresh mozzarella, basil leaves, and a drizzle of balsamic glaze. Arrange them on a platter for a visually stunning and appetizing hors d'oeuvre.

Greek Orzo Salad

Greek Orzo Salad is a crowd-pleasing dish that combines orzo pasta with cherry tomatoes, cucumber, Kalamata olives, red onion, and crumbled feta cheese. Toss it in a lemony Greek dressing for a tangy and refreshing salad that's perfect for celebrations.

Spinach and Strawberry Salad

A Spinach and Strawberry Salad brings together baby spinach leaves, fresh strawberries, sliced almonds, and crumbled goat cheese. Drizzle it with a sweet and tangy balsamic vinaigrette for a salad that's both vibrant and delectable.

Watermelon and Mint Salad

For a refreshing and visually striking option, consider a Watermelon and Mint Salad. It features cubes of sweet watermelon, fresh mint leaves, crumbled feta cheese, and a drizzle of extra virgin olive oil. This salad is a delightful balance of sweet and savory.

Lobster and Avocado Salad

For an indulgent and elegant option, serve Lobster and Avocado Salad. It combines tender lobster meat, creamy avocado slices, mixed greens, and a lemon-tarragon dressing. This salad is a luxurious choice for special occasions.

Picnic and Potluck Favorites

When you're planning a picnic or potluck gathering, Mediterranean salads are convenient and portable options. Here are some Mediterranean-inspired salads that are perfect for outdoor gatherings:

Greek Pasta Salad

Greek Pasta Salad is a picnic favorite. It features cooked pasta (such as rotini or penne) tossed with cherry tomatoes, cucumber, red onion, Kalamata olives, and crumbled feta cheese. The dressing combines extra virgin olive oil, lemon juice, and Greek spices for a zesty kick.

Mediterranean Couscous Salad

Mediterranean Couscous Salad is a quick and easy dish to prepare for a potluck. It includes cooked couscous, diced bell peppers, cherry tomatoes, cucumber, and fresh parsley. Drizzle it with a lemony dressing for a light and flavorful salad.

Quinoa Tabbouleh

Quinoa Tabbouleh is a gluten-free and protein-rich salad that's perfect for picnics. It combines cooked quinoa with finely chopped fresh herbs, diced cucumber, cherry tomatoes, and red onion. The dressing is a tangy blend of lemon juice and extra virgin olive oil.

Mediterranean Chickpea Salad Wraps

For a portable option, prepare Mediterranean Chickpea Salad Wraps. The salad features chickpeas, diced bell peppers, red onion, Kalamata olives, and crumbled feta cheese. Toss it in a lemon-tahini dressing and wrap it in whole-grain tortillas for easy picnic enjoyment.

Tuna Salad Niçoise

Tuna Salad Niçoise is a classic and hearty option for outdoor gatherings. It includes seared tuna steaks, boiled potatoes, green beans, cherry tomatoes, hard-boiled eggs, and Kalamata olives. Drizzle it with a Dijon vinaigrette for a satisfying meal.

Whether you're celebrating a special occasion or enjoying a casual picnic, these Mediterranean-inspired salads are sure to please and impress your guests.

Chapter 15: Mediterranean Salad Etiquette

Cultural Considerations

When enjoying Mediterranean salads, it's important to be mindful of cultural considerations to fully appreciate the dining experience. Here are some tips on Mediterranean salad etiquette:

Sharing and Generosity

Generosity: Mediterranean culture often emphasizes generosity in serving food. When hosting or dining with others, don't be surprised if portions are ample, and second helpings are encouraged.

Sharing: Sharing food is a common practice. It's customary to offer a taste of your salad to others at the table, especially if you're enjoying a meal in a social setting.

Use of Bread

Bread as a Utensil: In some Mediterranean cultures, it's common to use a piece of bread as a utensil to scoop up salad or other dishes. This is a practical and eco-friendly way to enjoy your meal.

Tearing, Not Cutting: If you choose to use bread, tear it into smaller pieces rather than cutting it with a knife. Cutting bread with a knife is considered impolite in some Mediterranean cultures.

Pace of Dining

Leisurely Dining: Mediterranean dining is often a leisurely affair. Take your time to savor each bite, engage in conversation, and enjoy the company of your dining companions.

No Rush: Don't rush through your meal. Meals are seen as opportunities to connect, relax, and appreciate the flavors and textures of the food.

Salad as a Starter

Salad as an Appetizer: In many Mediterranean countries, salad is often served as a starter before the main course. It's a way to whet the appetite and prepare the palate for the rest of the meal.

Follow the Order: When dining out, follow the order of courses as presented on the menu. If salad is listed as an appetizer, it's typically intended to be enjoyed before the main dish.

Salad as a Main Course

In Mediterranean cuisine, salads can take center stage as main courses. Here's how to embrace salads as satisfying and nutritious main dishes:

Protein-Packed Options

Include Protein: To make a salad a substantial main course, include protein-rich ingredients like grilled chicken, shrimp, tuna, chickpeas, or tofu. These additions provide satiety and balance.

Balanced Nutrition: Ensure your main course salad includes a variety of components, such as greens, vegetables, proteins, healthy fats, and grains. This balance ensures you get a well-rounded meal.

Diverse Flavors and Textures

Flavorful Components: Incorporate diverse flavors and textures to keep your salad exciting. Include sweet, savory, creamy, and crunchy elements. For example, mix fruits, nuts, and cheeses.

Dressing Matters

Well-Seasoned Dressing: The dressing plays a crucial role in enhancing the overall flavor of the salad. Choose a well-seasoned dressing that complements the ingredients. Options like Lemon-Tahini, Balsamic Olive Oil, or Pomegranate Vinaigrette can elevate your salad.

Sauce or Dressing on the Side: If you prefer to control the amount of dressing, ask for it on the side when dining out. You can then add it to your taste.

Lighter Options: opt for lighter dressings or vinaigrettes if you're conscious of calorie intake. A simple drizzle of extra virgin olive oil and lemon juice can also be delightful.

Enjoying Mediterranean salads as main courses allows you to explore a wide range of flavors and ingredients while maintaining a focus on health and balance. Embrace the variety and creativity that Mediterranean cuisine offers.

Chapter 16: Salads for Health and Wellness

The Mediterranean Diet and Health Benefits

The Mediterranean diet is renowned for its health benefits and is characterized by an abundance of fresh, whole foods. Mediterranean salads are a delicious and nutritious way to incorporate this dietary pattern into your life. Here are some of the health benefits associated with the Mediterranean diet:

Heart Health

Olive Oil: The use of extra virgin olive oil in Mediterranean cooking is linked to lower rates of heart disease. Its monounsaturated fats are heart-healthy and reduce the risk of cardiovascular problems.

Omega-3 Fatty Acids: Fish, a staple in Mediterranean cuisine, is rich in omega-3 fatty acids. These fats help reduce inflammation and lower the risk of heart disease.

Weight Management

Plant-Based Emphasis: The diet places a strong emphasis on fruits, vegetables, legumes, and whole grains, which are high in fiber and keep you feeling full, aiding in weight management.

Moderate Portions: The Mediterranean approach encourages mindful eating and portion control, promoting a healthy weight.

Diabetes Management

Low Glycemic Index: Mediterranean foods have a low glycemic index, meaning they don't cause rapid spikes in blood sugar levels. This helps in managing and preventing diabetes.

Antioxidant-Rich

Colorful Produce: The diet is rich in colorful fruits and vegetables, providing a wide range of antioxidants that protect cells from damage.

Reduced Inflammation

Fatty Fish and Nuts: The consumption of fatty fish and nuts contributes to lower levels of inflammation in the body.

Weight Management with Mediterranean Salads

Mediterranean salads can be an excellent tool for weight management due to their balanced and nutrient-rich ingredients. Here are some tips for using Mediterranean salads to support your weight goals:

Portion Control

Mindful Eating: Pay attention to portion sizes. While Mediterranean salads are healthy, consuming them in excessive quantities can lead to calorie surplus.

Smaller Plates: Consider using smaller plates when serving salads to help control portion sizes.

Balance Macronutrients

Protein: Include protein sources like grilled chicken, shrimp, chickpeas, or tofu to keep you feeling full and satisfied.

Healthy Fats: Embrace healthy fats from sources like extra virgin olive oil, nuts, and avocado, but be mindful of portion sizes.

Limit High-Calorie Ingredients

Cheese: While feta and other cheeses are delicious, use them in moderation due to their calorie content.

Dressing: Use dressing in moderation and consider lighter options like vinaigrettes.

High-Fiber Ingredients

Leafy Greens: Base your salad on leafy greens, as they're low in calories but high in fiber and nutrients.

Legumes: Incorporate legumes like chickpeas or lentils for added fiber and protein.

Regular Physical Activity

Exercise: Complement your Mediterranean salad-based diet with regular physical activity to achieve your weight management goals.

Hydration

Water: Stay hydrated throughout the day by drinking plenty of water, as thirst can sometimes be mistaken for hunger.

Dietary Restrictions and Adaptations

Mediterranean salads are versatile and can be adapted to various dietary restrictions and preferences. Here are some adaptations for specific dietary needs:

Vegetarian and Vegan Options

Plant-Based Proteins: Replace animal proteins with plant-based options like tofu, tempeh, or a variety of beans and legumes.

Nutritional Yeast: Use nutritional yeast as a dairy-free alternative for a cheesy flavor.

Dressings: Choose dairy-free dressings or make your own with ingredients like tahini, balsamic vinegar, or lemon juice.

Gluten-Free

Grain Alternatives: Substitute gluten-containing grains with gluten-free options like quinoa, rice, or gluten-free pasta.

Low-Carb

Limit Grains: Reduce or eliminate grains and focus on leafy greens, vegetables, and protein sources for a low-carb salad.

Healthy Fats: Increase the use of healthy fats like extra virgin olive oil and avocado to add richness to your low-carb salad.

Allergies

Ingredient Substitutions: If you have allergies, substitute ingredients you can't consume with suitable alternatives. For example, use sunflower seeds instead of nuts.

Read Labels: When using pre-made ingredients like dressings or cheeses, carefully read labels to ensure they don't contain allergens.

Adapting Mediterranean salads to your dietary preferences and restrictions allows you to enjoy the benefits of this nutritious cuisine while staying true to your health goals.

Chapter 17: Kids and Family-Friendly Salads

Getting Kids to Love Veggies

Encouraging children to embrace vegetables can be a delightful journey. Mediterranean salads offer a range of colorful and flavorful options that can make veggies more appealing to kids. Here are some strategies to get kids excited about veggies:

1. Involve Kids in the Process

Grocery Shopping: Bring your kids along when you go grocery shopping. Let them choose a few vegetables they'd like to try.

Meal Preparation: Involve kids in preparing salads. They can wash, peel, or chop vegetables (with supervision) and participate in assembling salads.

2. Make It Fun

Colorful Creations: Create colorful salads by using a variety of veggies. Challenge kids to make a rainbow salad with different colored vegetables.

Shapes and Sizes: Use cookie cutters to cut vegetables into fun shapes. For example, cucumber stars or carrot hearts can make veggies more appealing.

Build Your Own Salad: Set up a "salad bar" with various salad ingredients, and let kids build their own salads. They love having control over what goes into their bowl.

3. Add Familiar Flavors

Dip It: Serve vegetables with a tasty dip like hummus, tzatziki, or yogurt-based dressing. Kids often enjoy dipping veggies into flavorful sauces.

Cheese Please: A sprinkle of mild cheese like feta or mozzarella can make veggies more enticing.

4. Hide Veggies

Blend into Dressings: Sneak vegetables like spinach, carrots, or bell peppers into homemade salad dressings. Kids won't even notice, and it adds extra nutrition.

Pasta Salads: Mix finely chopped veggies into pasta salads. The pasta distracts from the vegetables, and kids get used to the flavors.

Fun and Creative Salad Ideas

Mediterranean salads can be transformed into fun and creative dishes that kids will adore. Here are some playful salad ideas:

1. Mediterranean Pasta Salad Skewers

Thread cooked pasta, cherry tomatoes, cucumber slices, and mozzarella balls onto skewers. Drizzle with a light dressing and serve as pasta salad skewers. Kids love eating food off skewers.

2. Greek Salad Wraps

Wrap Greek salad ingredients in a whole-grain tortilla or pita bread. Add a dollop of tzatziki sauce, roll it up, and slice into bite-sized pinwheels.

3. Ants on a Log Salad

Make a healthier version of the classic "ants on a log" snack. Fill celery sticks with hummus or cream cheese, then top with diced bell peppers, cherry tomatoes, and raisins. The colorful veggies resemble "ants" on a log.

4. Mediterranean Pizza Salad

Create a deconstructed Mediterranean pizza salad by arranging cherry tomatoes, olives, and feta cheese on a plate. Drizzle with balsamic glaze to mimic pizza sauce.

5. Fruit and Veggie Butterfly Salad

Cut cucumber slices into butterfly shapes and arrange them on a plate. Use grapes or cherry tomatoes for the body and add colorful fruit and vegetable "wings."

Family Mealtime Traditions

Family mealtime traditions are a wonderful way to connect and create lasting memories. Mediterranean salads can be a central part of these traditions. Here are some ideas:

1. Salad Sundays

Designate Sundays as "Salad Sundays." Gather the family to prepare and enjoy a variety of Mediterranean salads together. Rotate who gets to choose the salad recipes each week.

2. Salad Challenge

Have a "Salad Challenge" where each family member takes turns inventing their own salad creation. They can select ingredients and make a unique dressing. Taste and rate each other's salads.

3. Outdoor Picnics

Plan outdoor picnics in your backyard or local park. Mediterranean salads are perfect for picnic spreads. Enjoy your salads on a blanket and relish quality family time.

4. Family Cookbook

Create a family cookbook filled with your favorite Mediterranean salad recipes. Let each family member contribute their own salad recipe and a story about why they love it.

5. Cooking Together

Cooking together can be a bonding experience. Assign family members different roles in preparing a Mediterranean salad, from chopping vegetables to mixing dressings. The final result is a collaborative creation.

Mediterranean salads can be a bridge to family togetherness, promoting a love for fresh, healthy foods, and creating cherished mealtime traditions.

Chapter 18: Mediterranean Salad Challenges

Troubleshooting Tips

Even the most seasoned home cooks encounter challenges when preparing salads. Here are some troubleshooting tips to overcome common issues when making Mediterranean salads:

1. Overdressed Salad

Issue: Your salad is overly soggy or drowned in dressing.

Solution:

Add More Greens: If your salad is too wet, toss in additional greens to absorb the excess dressing.

Drain and Toss: If the dressing has pooled at the bottom of the bowl, drain it off and toss the salad again with a lighter hand.

Use Tongs: When tossing the salad, use tongs or salad servers instead of a spoon to distribute the dressing evenly without overpouring.

2. Bland Flavor

Issue: Your salad lacks flavor and excitement.

Solution:

Season Generously: Don't be shy with seasonings. Add salt, freshly ground black pepper, and herbs like basil, mint, or parsley to enhance the taste.

Acid Kick: A dash of lemon juice or vinegar can brighten up a lackluster salad.

Cheese Boost: If appropriate, add crumbled feta, goat cheese, or Parmesan for a salty and savory kick.

3. Soggy Ingredients

Issue: Your salad ingredients, like cucumbers or tomatoes, have become soggy.

Solution:

Use Fresh Ingredients: Start with fresh and firm vegetables to prevent sogginess. Avoid bruised or overripe produce.

Seed Removal: For ingredients like tomatoes and cucumbers, remove seeds and excess moisture to keep them crisp.

Last-Minute Addition: Add delicate ingredients like sliced avocado or herbs just before serving to maintain their freshness.

4. Wilting Greens

Issue: Your greens have wilted and lost their crispness.

Solution:

Refrigerate Properly: Store greens in the crisper drawer of your refrigerator in a breathable bag or container to extend their shelf life.

Ice Bath: If your greens have wilted, submerge them in a bowl of ice water for a few minutes, then pat them dry to revive their crispness.

Avoid Pre-Dressing: Don't dress the salad until just before serving to prevent greens from wilting prematurely.

Handling Leftovers

Mediterranean salads often taste even better the next day as flavors meld together. Here's how to handle leftovers effectively:

Refrigeration: Store leftover salad in an airtight container in the refrigerator. If possible, separate the dressing from the salad to prevent sogginess.

Protein Preservation: If your salad contains protein like grilled chicken or seafood, store it separately to maintain its texture and prevent it from becoming dry.

Use Within Days: Consume leftover salads within 2-3 days to ensure freshness and food safety.

Refresh: If the salad seems a bit dry the next day, add a drizzle of fresh dressing and toss to revive the flavors.

Storing Salad Ingredients

Properly storing salad ingredients helps extend their freshness and ensures your salads taste their best:

Leafy Greens: Store greens in the crisper drawer of your refrigerator. Place a paper towel in the bag or container to absorb excess moisture and prevent wilting.

Fresh Herbs: Place fresh herbs in a glass of water, similar to a bouquet, and cover them with a plastic bag. Keep them in the refrigerator for extended freshness.

Cucumbers and Tomatoes: Store these ingredients on the countertop, away from direct sunlight, until they're ripe. Once ripe, move them to the refrigerator to extend their shelf life.

Fruits: Store fruits like strawberries and grapes in the refrigerator, but bring them to room temperature before adding them to salads to enhance their flavor.

Dressing: Keep homemade dressings in a sealed container in the refrigerator. Store store-bought dressings according to the manufacturer's instructions.

By troubleshooting common salad issues, handling leftovers wisely, and storing salad ingredients properly, you can enjoy delicious and satisfying Mediterranean salads with ease.

Conclusion and Beyond

Mediterranean Salad Revolution

Congratulations on embarking on your Mediterranean salad journey! You've discovered the vibrant flavors, health benefits, and versatility of Mediterranean salads. By now, you're well-equipped to create and enjoy a wide array of delicious salads inspired by the Mediterranean region.

Your Journey Continues

As you continue your culinary adventure, remember that the world of Mediterranean salads is vast and ever-evolving. Don't hesitate to experiment, tweak recipes to suit your preferences, and discover new ingredients and combinations. The Mediterranean diet offers a lifetime of exploration and enjoyment.

Share your love for Mediterranean salads with family and friends, and encourage them to join you on this flavorful and healthful journey. Whether it's a casual weeknight dinner or a special celebration, Mediterranean salads have a place at every table.

Thank you for joining us on this Mediterranean salad adventure. We hope this cookbook has inspired your culinary creativity and encouraged a deeper appreciation for the delicious and nutritious world of Mediterranean salads.

Bon appétit, and here's to many more flavorful salads in your future!

9 798223 306221